D1603780

PHIL HELLMUTH JR.

#POSITIVITY

YOU ARE ALWAYS IN THE RIGHT PLACE AT THE RIGHT TIME

8 TIPS FOR SUCCESS

PHIL HELLMUTH JR.

#POSITIVITY

YOU ARE ALWAYS IN THE RIGHT PLACE
AT THE RIGHT TIME

8 LIFE TIPS

Published by Phil Hellmuth

Copyright 2018 © Phil Hellmuth Services

Paperback ISBN: 978-1-936549-00-9

Digital ISBN: 978-1-936549-01-6

Cover: Dino Marino

Interior Design: Christina Gorchos, 3CsBooks.com

ACKNOWLEDGEMENTS

Mom, thank you for putting me on the path to positivity! Your unrelenting belief in me, when there was no evidence to support your rosy opinion of me, contributed heavily to my successes. Dad, thank you for teaching me the importance of perfect ethics and honor. And for your solid advice and steady hand...

DEDICATION

To my wife Kathy; thank you for making
me a better man.

TABLE OF CONTENTS

YOU'RE INVITED

I'd like to invite you to connect with me at

PhilHellmuthsPOSITIVITY.com

Grab resources, and stay updated with
exciting events, news, and advice from the
book. I look forward to connecting and
hearing about your journey!

INTRODUCTION

When I was a child, my mother taped a sign to our bathroom mirror that read:

> *You are what you think;*
> *You become what you think;*
> *What you think becomes reality.*

Every morning for ten years, my siblings and I—all five of us—read that sign. With every trip to the bathroom, I'd see those same three lines over and over again.

Eventually, the square of paper would become faded and worn, and my mom would simply replace it with a new one. New piece of paper, same message. I saw that sign thousands of times during my adolescent years—so many times I felt like I saw it in my sleep.

But for all the exposure to my mom's message, I was struggling. My high school years were tough. I had trouble focusing. I had trouble making friends. I had trouble meeting girls. I had trouble with grades. At times, it seemed like I had trouble with almost everything.

But through it all, I kept seeing my mom's little sign.

It began to dawn on me that if my mom's message was true—if the way I *thought* was creating who I *was*—then perhaps I needed to change how I thought. If I wanted things to be different, I reasoned, my *thinking* needed to be different.

And so it was, with each trip to that shared family bathroom, my mom's little sign began to shape the way I looked at life.

Little did I know at the time that those three lines held the key to my future success. Over the years they became the foundation for how I approached my career, my relationships, and my entire life. From one scrap of paper, a philosophy was born.

And it paid off.

In 1989, at the age of 24, I became the youngest person ever to win the World Series of Poker Main Event. Many more victories followed, and on the road to becoming the best poker player in the world, a New York Times best-selling author (*Play Poker like the Pros*), a television host, a political writer (for Street.com), and a global poker icon, I refined that philosophy. I learned, then mastered, the techniques that helped fuel my rise to the top of the mountain. Once I reached the top, I used those same techniques to stay there.

Around 2011 I began using the hashtag POSITIVITY in social media, and began to further distill my thinking into a philosophy that I could share with others.

Now, more than 40 years since I first saw my mom's determined little bathroom sign, the entire philosophy of #POSITIVITY is right here, in this book.

#POSITIVITY contains eight simple yet powerful techniques that I've used to reach the top of my career and stay there. My motivation for sharing them is clear to me: I want to inspire the world. I want to help propel millions of people along the path toward their dreams—whether that's to make more money, start a business, gain more independence, acquire a more positive attitude, lose weight, or clear positive space in their lives by forgiving their enemies.

You don't become the world's greatest poker player without making some big bets. My big wager now is that *#POSITIVITY* will help every person who reads it.

In this book, I'll show you:

- The folly in hating others and the wisdom in forgiving them.

- The power of yearly goals and how, following my mom's lead, I nurtured and supported my own climb to the top by taping my yearly goals to my bathroom mirror.

- How to write up your "Pyramid of Success." I wrote my own pyramid way back in 1988, and I stick to it to this day.

- How "we are all in the right place at the right time" and how to be ready for those serendipitous moments.

- How to "take the first step"—that critical first action toward your goals and dreams. It's of utmost importance, and many of us fall short because we never take it.

- How to keep your ego under control and your head down after you achieve success. If I can help put you on the path to success, you'll need to learn how to deal with it.

Decades after my mom's little sign appeared in our family bathroom, the #POSITIVITY philosophy has transformed my life.

- √ I thought that I could become a great poker player; *check*.

- √ I thought that I could write a *New York Times* best-selling book; *check*.

- √ I thought that I could buy a beautiful house; *check*.

- √ I thought that I could meet and marry a wonderful woman; *check* (28 years and counting!).

- √ I thought I could be a loving father and raise good, strong, and fair children; *check*.

√ And I think that I can help you, and millions of others, to achieve more in your life! *Check*.

Welcome to *#POSITIVITY*. Let's get started.

Phil Hellmuth
PALO ALTO, CA
JANUARY 2018

CHAPTER ONE

WRITE DOWN YOUR LIFE GOALS

On a cold and bleak March morning in 1988, I headed out for a weekly poker game. I had dropped out of school a little more than a year earlier to play professionally, and I was in love with the game. I'd recently come off some winning trips to Vegas, and I felt I was hitting my stride as a professional poker player.

That morning, however, was one of those grey Wisconsin winter days, devoid of sun, and it mirrored my mood. I felt restless and unsettled. I simply didn't want to be playing poker that morning, but I couldn't quite put my finger on why.

By noon, just an hour into the game, I found myself wanting to leave. Maybe the stakes of the game were a little too small for me after my experiences in Vegas, or perhaps I was just burned out. In any case, I found myself craving the outdoors. I told myself, *I've just spent too much time playing poker indoors over the last few weeks.*

I finally convinced two of the seven players to leave the game with me. We smoked some pot, then drove to a bar down the road. When we arrived, we ordered drinks and began playing pool, first for $10 a game, and then for $20. Still, I was frustrated with the action. I was the worst pool player in the group and I couldn't get a fair game; even if I could, the stakes were too modest. I thought,

Why bother? What a waste of time. What am I even doing here?

I SEE THE LIGHT

As I was preparing to leave, I noticed a side door across the room. I walked over and opened it, and sunlight flooded into the bar. As my bleary eyes adjusted to the white light that streamed over me, I gazed out over the beautiful snowy landscape and the busy street that fronted the bar. The snow on the side of the road was still a foot deep, lying in half-melted, icy piles.

The sunlight—so unexpected on an overcast day—was a shock to my system. It was as if I "woke up" from my life and was startled to realize where I was, and what I was doing.

Why, exactly, was I standing here? What was I doing with my life? With a jolt, the reality of what I was doing struck home: Here I was, in a bar having a drink, after I had smoked pot … and it was *noon*. You may have heard the song by the Talking Heads, "Once in a Lifetime." I felt like the man in the song— like I had just woken up years into my life and was now asking myself, *How did I get here?* It was a profound sense of becoming *aware*, as if I'd just woken up and was only now seeing that my poker life had become a tedious nightmare.

I made some excuses to my friends, called a taxi, and got out of there *fast*.

PUTTING PEN TO PAPER

I felt anxious the whole cab ride home, desperately wanting to grab on to this moment of energy and clarity before it slipped away. I felt, as the Talking Heads' song suggested, that this might really be a once-in-a-lifetime moment.

As soon as I walked into my apartment, I sat down at my desk, pulled out a pen and some paper, and asked myself one question: *What, exactly, am I going to do with my life?*

Drawing on the energy of my sunlight-fueled awakening, I wrote the following:

LIFE GOALS

1. *Win the Main Event at the WSOP (World Series of Poker).*

2. *Meet and marry a wonderful woman, one who can abide me.*

3. *Write a* New York Times *best-selling book.*

4. *Buy a beautiful house.*

5. *Buy a beautiful car.*

6. *Win tons of big poker tournaments.*

I wanted to capture the moment—to think big and reach for the stars—and use it to fuel my path forward. And it worked. Two years later, in 1990, my wife Kathy found the list and read through it. "That's amazing," she exclaimed. "You've already accomplished a bunch of your life goals!" It wasn't long before I'd accomplished *all* of them.

Most of our life goals aren't achieved overnight. It took until 2003 for me to write my first book, and in 2004 *Play Poker Like the Pros* hit the *New York Times* bestseller list (check!). But that's part of the beauty of goals and of #POSITIVITY—everything can be a work in progress. There's always something else to discover or to accomplish.

In May 1993, I added a huge goal to my life list: to become the greatest poker player of all time. I now have a record fourteen WSOP wins—second place has ten. If I can win 24 WSOP tournaments, I feel that will be enough for me to be considered the greatest poker player of all time.

WHAT'S ON YOUR LIST?

That winter day in Wisconsin, something shifted in me; I began to think bigger, and I began to capture that thinking on paper. You should as well! Why *not* reach for the stars?

Why not start this second? Take the first step and write down a rough draft of your list immediately. You don't have to be perfect, and you don't have to capture everything. You can revise the list tomorrow. In fact, you can revise the list anytime that you like. Writing down your life goals isn't something that you pull off in one day and then forget about. You can have as many lifetime goals on your list as feels comfortable to you—whether that's one goal or fifteen or more.

I believe that writing a list of life goals is an essential ingredient in reaching serious levels of success—it's one of the single most powerful actions you can take toward reaching your dreams. Writing down your goals gives you something clear and precise to go after. Otherwise, how will you know exactly what you want to accomplish in your life? I recommend that you pull out your Life Goals list once or twice a month, and use it as a compass to guide you where you want to go.

CHAPTER TWO

"BATHROOM MIRROR" YOUR YEARLY GOALS

My Life Goals list from the previous chapter is extremely important—it not only captures the energy of my life when I feel at my best, but it gives my life direction and purpose. Without it, it would be easy to feel adrift, like I did on that winter day at the bar.

I don't look at that list constantly. But I do pull it out regularly to touch base with my purpose, and to make sure I'm on track. I do, however, see my *yearly* goals list every single day, because—no surprise—it's taped to my bathroom mirror.

My Yearly Goals list is shorter-term—it covers just one calendar year. But it helps guide me toward achieving the larger, lifetime goals that might take longer to reach, or require more steps.

Each year I change my Yearly Goals list, but there are some constants. For example, I always have the lofty goal of winning three World Series of Poker tournaments on my Yearly Goals list, and this feeds into my *lifetime* goal of becoming the greatest poker player of all time. For me, accomplishing that lifetime goal means winning 24 WSOP bracelets. The annual goal of winning three is a way of moving me steadily closer.

Each day, when I brush my teeth or put on deodorant, I see my Yearly Goals list right there on the bathroom mirror. Most days I don't consciously read it. Most of the time, I don't even consciously *notice* it.

But unconsciously, I know it's there and it informs my day even if I'm not aware of it.

Here's a recent Yearly Goals list:

YEARLY GOALS

1. Win 3 World Series of Poker bracelets

2. Win 2 World Poker Tour tournaments

3. Make my autobiography *Poker Brat* hit the *New York Times* bestseller list

4. Get good time with Kathy, Phillip, Nick

5. Get good time with my best friends Chamath and Bill and their families

6. Sign a few big contracts!

7. Walk 10,000 steps a day

8. Finish my next book *#POSITIVITY*

9. Get the television show *Lodden Thinks* greenlit (I will produce and co-star)

10. Raise money for OR help grow Kimo Sabe Mezcal, Muzik One Headphones, Essential Phones, and BlitzPredict

When I look back on that list now, I can see that I made great progress on most of my goals. Without the list, I'd have no way of knowing exactly how much I'd accomplished.

CREATE YOUR YEARLY GOALS LIST

My call to action to you right now is simple: write down a list of your yearly goals. Start the list *this minute*—do it on your phone, on a blank piece of paper near you, or even on the back of a napkin. Just do it!

Start by writing at the top, in big letters *Yearly Goals*. Include the current calendar year. Don't worry about perfection—just write your goals down, in no particular order. When you have more time, you can edit the list, putting the most important yearly goals at the top, and the least important ones at the bottom. For now, just focus on capturing them in one place.

When you have more time, here are some tips for improving your list:

- Consider making your list digital. That makes it easy to edit, and it means you can print out extra copies as required.

- Edit the list so that it fits conveniently on one piece of paper. I always make the title bigger than the rest of the type.

- Make sure the list is exactly how you want it—you're going to be seeing a lot of it! I put the most important yearly goals at the top.

- Choose a reasonable number. I choose ten goals in part because that was the most I could comfortably fit on one sheet of paper, and also because ten just seemed like enough.

- Make two copies of your Yearly Goals list, and tape one of those paper copies to your bathroom mirror. Place the other copy where you have continual access to it. I take the other copy of my list on the road with me wherever I go. For example, I will tape my Yearly Goals list to the bathroom mirror at the ARIA Resort & Casino, where I might stay for two months at a time during the WSOP. You can leave the extra copy of your list in your backpack or briefcase, on your desk, or wherever makes the most sense to you.

Your Yearly Goals list can't help you if you don't write it down. Don't worry about getting it right—just get it written! And when you're done ... onto the bathroom mirror it goes!

You can download one of my videos at:

www.PhilHellmuthsPOSITIVITY.com

CHAPTER THREE

"BATHROOM MIRROR" YOUR BLESSINGS

S ide-by-side with the Yearly Goals list on my bathroom mirror is another piece of paper. I call it my *Blessings List*. It's a list of things I'm grateful for.

In the morning, while I'm brushing my teeth or combing my hair, I can clearly see what I want to accomplish—my yearly goals are right there in front of me. But by gazing inches to the right, I can also check out my Blessings List. When I leave the washroom,

I'm more aware of what I'm trying to accomplish, but I'm also happy and thankful for what I already have.

Here's my current list of Blessings :

BLESSINGS

"Rejoice every day and be thankful."
—PRESIDENT JOHN ADAMS

1. Great health for me

2. Great health for my family

3. Kathy, Phillip, and Nick

4. 14 World Series of Poker bracelets

5. Great friends

6. Fame and fortune

7. My *New York Times* best-selling book *Play Poker Like the Pros*

8. A beautiful house

9. My books *Poker Brat* and *#POSITIVITY*

10. Great sponsorships, advisory board deals, and deals

Every single morning, I consciously—or unconsciously—see this list of Blessings taped to my bathroom mirror, and I leave the house happier, having been reminded on some level that I've been blessed.

GREAT HEALTH AND FAMILY TOP THE LIST

My health isn't perfect—I have sleep apnea and GERD (gastroesophageal reflux disease)—but at age 53, I still feel my health is excellent. Sleep apnea affects over 20% of the world; if you snore at night, there's a 98% that you have it. I've used a breathing machine for ten years, without missing a night. The machine holds sleep apnea at bay, and I'm lucky to be living in this age, and not 40 years ago, when sleep apnea could have taken a decade off my life span.

GERD is not a big deal either—it seems to hit people when they turn 50 (President Obama and I both came down with it close to our fiftieth birthdays). With GERD, I simply avoid eating too much food in one meal, and avoid eating too many fatty foods in one sitting.

Neither one of these issues interferes with my life significantly. I'm still very grateful—without good health, life becomes a lot harder. Health is the one blessing that allows me to enjoy all the other ones in my life. After years of writing up my list of blessings, I can absolutely say that great health belongs at the very top!

Great health for my family, and just the fact that I *have* a family (a terrific wife and two honorable sons), make up the next two spots of my Blessings list. Family ranks above even my number one lifetime achievement, my 14 World Series of Poker wins. In the end, your family will be there for you. My health, my family, and their health, top my Blessings list.

WRITE DOWN YOUR OWN LIST OF BLESSINGS NOW

It's time for action. Write down your own list of blessings right now. The order doesn't matter—just write them down. Write until you've gotten everything you can think of, but don't worry about being perfect. You can always come back and edit the list later when you have more time.

You can call your list anything you want. If you prefer the term "gratitude," use that. You can just call your list "Things I'm Thankful For." The label doesn't matter—it's writing it down that makes the difference.

If you're having trouble coming up with blessings, just remember that many people in this world are starving, struggling, and facing tough situations. They're unemployed, sick, or living with the constant threat of danger. If you think beyond yourself, you don't have to look far to find something to be grateful for.

Once you've finished writing, put the list away and come back to it later to make revisions:

- As with your goals, consider making a digital version of your list so you can easily edit it and print out extra copies.

- A list of blessings that fits comfortably onto one page works best.

- Put the biggest blessings at the top of your Blessings list. Your eyes naturally tend to migrate to top of any list or page that you read.

- I recommend that you make the font size at the top bigger than the font size that you use for your numbered blessings.

- I like to have an inspirational quote at the top of my list. Right now, I use the President John Adams quote "Rejoice every day and be thankful."

When you're satisfied with your Blessings, print them out and tape it on your bathroom mirror, right next to your Yearly Goals list.

With your Blessings list now securely hanging where you can see it every day, I'll wager that you will leave your home with more positivity in your step!

CHAPTER FOUR

CREATE YOUR PYRAMID FOR SUCCESS

The winter day when I "woke up" from my dreary existence to ponder what I was going to do with my life led to more than just clarifying and writing down my life goals.

I loved poker, and I was good at it. But I figured if I was going to continue playing, then I might as well work towards becoming not just a good player, but a great one—maybe the best in the world. Why not?

To get there, however, I knew I'd have to do more than just write down the goal. I'd have to figure out exactly what I had to do to get there. To become a great poker player, there were key skills that I'd have to master. I'd already seen—and personally experienced—what happens when you don't have all the skills in place to play at the top of your game. If I wanted to be great, I knew I'd have to learn to master each one.

THE WINNING PYRAMID

As I pondered the skills I needed to reach the top, I came up with a concept I call the *Winning Pyramid*. I took all the necessary building blocks needed to achieve world-class success in poker, and structured them in a way that was not only easy to understand, but also created a hierarchy to show what skills were most important.

The pyramid was a triangle made from ten blocks, with each block representing a key skill I needed to master. I listed them in order of importance, with the bottom being the least important, and easiest to implement (at least for me personally), and the top being the most important, but also the most challenging to master.

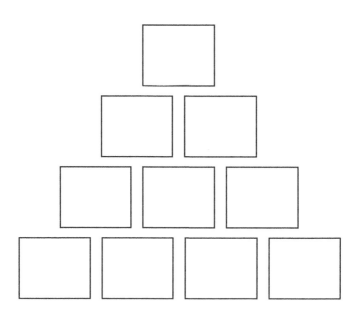

THE WINNING PYRAMID

Each row contained skills that were related, so that each level of the pyramid represented an overall strategy as well.

ROW 1: AVOID LEAKS

On the bottom row of the pyramid, I put the biggest leaks. In poker, a *leak* is a trap, like playing craps, that drains cash from your bankroll. Leaks can destroy a poker career, but many poker players still seem to tolerate them. In order to build and maintain the funds I needed to play, I'd have to avoid leaks. The bottom row of my pyramid became : *avoid casino games*, *avoid sports betting*, *avoid drugs*, and *avoid alcohol in excess*.

ROW 2: BUILD GREAT HEALTH

Just as health tops my list of blessings, it's important in the pyramid, too. Professional poker competition is a marathon. Games can last for hours, and without great health, you lose your ability to focus and make the right decisions when the stakes are high.

The next level up on my pyramid was dedicated to my health. I added *exercise*, *eat healthfully*, and *get proper rest*. I try to stay healthy and to not play poker when I'm tired.

ROW 3: STAY OFF TILT

Poker players use the expression *on tilt* to describe an emotional state, like anger, or frustration, in which they have a tendency to make bad decisions or play poorly. It's very easy to lose control at the tables when you're emotionally on tilt.

On the third level up of my winning pyramid, I added *maintain emotional control*, which for me means having the ability to avoid pressing in the moment, as well as *be disciplined*, which means to play the game with great patience in the long run, over *all* of my future poker sessions.

TOP ROW: MANAGE MONEY

You can have all the poker talent in the world, but if you allow yourself to run out of money when a juicy game appears, then you'll be on the sidelines (probably watching less talented players pursue that amazing game). The only thing that can potentially trump talent at the poker table is the ability to be in control of your finances.

At the top of my winning pyramid I put *great money management.*

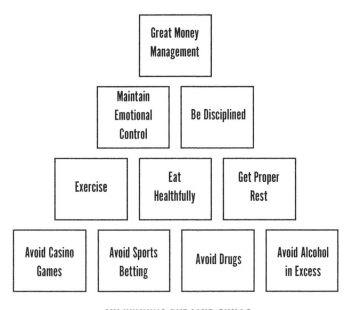

MY WINNING PYRAMID SKILLS

Creating my pyramid was a turning point in my life. I had already written down my life goals and for the first time I clearly understood where I wanted to go and who I wanted to be. Now, with the Winning Pyramid, I knew exactly how to get there.

Moreover, the pyramid turned out to be valuable in almost *everything* I did. I used the Winning Pyramid for the next 29 years to win 14 World Series of Poker bracelets, but also to write a *New York Times* best-selling book, stay healthy, join advisory boards for companies like Muzik Headphones and BlitzPredict, and reach for the stars.

WRITE UP THE BLOCKS FOR YOUR OWN PYRAMID

If you've been following my calls to action in the previous chapters, then you've written down both your life goals and your yearly goals; you now have a good idea of what you want to do with your life. It's now time to clarify the skills you need to get there by designing your own Winning Pyramid.

Begin by taking a long and honest look at your weaknesses. Perhaps drinking alcohol in excess is an issue for you? Or drugs? Maybe you spend too much money or have trouble saving. Do you have trouble eating a healthy diet? Be honest and put these blocks in your pyramid. For example, you might write, *never have more than three drinks on any given day*, *save $200 a week*, or *eat a healthy diet* on your pyramid. As with poker, weaknesses and bad habits are leaks that can drain important resources from your life.

What else will you need to do to in order to make your goals a reality? What blocks need to be added to your pyramid of success? I'll wager that *be disciplined* and *get proper rest* are two of those building blocks—both are certainly two big keys to my success. And I'm sure *great money management* fits on your pyramid of success somewhere. Part of great money management is simply being able to pay your bills on time, and that provides an enormous sense of relief.

Personalize your pyramid to serve your goals. Be firm and honest with yourself. With your pyramid, don't worry about the next steps to achieve your goals, just focus on the skills you'll need to reach them.

WHY NOT BUILD YOUR PYRAMID NOW?

Sit down right now and create your own personalized pyramid for success! Build a pyramid that you can be proud of, one that captures (on a single page) all the skills you need to reach for the stars.

When I pull out my own Winning Pyramid (once a month or so), I study its rows. I ask myself: Have I managed to honor each block? At this point in my life, do I need to work on one (or more) of the skills?

Write up your pyramid of success, but don't worry about getting it exactly right the first time. Come back to it a few times if you need to. Once you're satisfied, tuck it away and pull that pyramid out as often as you like to stay on track. Or, if you prefer, tape it to your bathroom mirror—although that mirror might be little full already!

CHAPTER FIVE

HONOR YOUR CODE

t's one thing to never reach for the stars. But what if you reach and then miss your opportunity when it comes? As I climbed the poker ranks, I watched people melt at the tables when they had a chance to do something special. Faced with the opportunity to win a world championship or millions of dollars, they seemed to disintegrate right when they most needed to keep it together.

I always wondered, *Why do they fall apart?*

In 2001, I found out the hard way.

FALLING APART IN VEGAS

By the turn of the millennium, I was on a roll, and hard on the trail of my goal of becoming the greatest poker player of all time—the lifetime goal that I had first written down in 1993.

I knew that goal was tied heavily to the number of World Series of Poker bracelets I won, and my sights were firmly fixed on winning bracelets. After years of work, I was finally in a position to tie the record; I was on the cusp of becoming the all-time leader in WSOP wins.

As I described in *Poker Brat*, I had battled for years in a three-way bracelet race with pros Johnny Chan and Doyle Brunson. By the early 2000s, the race was dominating the poker headlines, and in the spring of 2001, I returned to Vegas for the WSOP.

I had seven bracelets, just one short of the record, and had come close several times to an eighth. Now, here I was, heads up with Scotty Nguyen, and I had a big chip lead. I was just a few hands away from tying the all-time bracelet record, and one step closer to becoming the "All-Time Greatest" in the poker world.

On the outside, I was playing it cool. This was poker, after all. Inside, things were beginning to go off the rails. With my goal within reach, I began to lose focus. I let my mind drift from the game in front of me, and thought, *You can take a huge step towards becoming the all-time great today.*

It wasn't unusual for me to think about that goal. I had been building my #POSITIVITY mindset for years—I knew where I was headed and the steps I needed to take to get there.

What *was* new was what happened next.

It was as if a new voice began to speak up in my head. *Do I deserve it?* the voice asked. *Have I paid my dues?*

The questions began to swirl through my mind. *Do I deserve to tie the bracelet leader Doyle Brunson, who probably could have had five more bracelets if he had tried solely for*

WSOP wins? Do I deserve to use all my God-given powers? Is it fair that I have skills like intuition, and the ability to read other people, and my opponents don't?

Eventually, I settled down, and put my mind back in the moment, on the game in front of me. Sadly, it was too late. I fell short that time around and lost to Scotty.

WHY WE FALL APART

After that upset, I began to think more about why people fall apart—why they choke or come up short when the stakes are high. The more I looked at those who crashed and burned under pressure, the more I began to see a common thread through all their stories. They tended to fall apart—often just mere hours away from mega-success—because they *lacked a sense of entitlement.*

It seems counter-intuitive. As a society, we've come to see entitlement as a bad thing—how could more of it lead to success?

For me, however, the opposite was true. I didn't understand how you could expect to succeed at a high level if you didn't believe you deserved to. When I looked around, it was clear to me that those who lacked entitlement simply felt that they didn't deserve more success than they already had. I believe that those who abused substances, were abusive to others, made bad decisions, or destroyed relationships would then self-destruct when their moment in the sun arrived. By making poor choices they drove their own self-esteem and sense of entitlement down, down, down.

If you want to be successful, you need a healthy sense of entitlement. The question is: *how do you get it?*

WHY NOT ME?

After the WSOP ended, I took a long look at what had happened to me in that record-tying moment and I asked myself, "Do I deserve to be the all-time greatest? Do I deserve to use all of the gifts that have been given to me?"

I wanted the answer to be yes. I *needed* the answer to be yes if I was going to reach my goals. So I sat down and began to build my case. Point by point, I began to list reasons why I felt I was deserving of success.

- I am loyal to my wife; I have never cheated on her.

- I have nearly perfect honor and ethics. I'm a man of my word.

- I am a good family man.

- I try to be inspiring. In 2001, a gentleman approached me to tell me that he had been in a coma, and had only survived because he thought about playing me heads up at poker! I am always inspired by watching my heroes, and hope to do the same for others.

- I am a good person. I try my best. I am honest and caring.

- I give money to my parents, my brother, and my sisters, and I give heavily to charities.

As I looked over the list, I realized that I had lived my life in alignment with my own strict code of honor. I'd been a good person, and supported many others along the way. I was, above all, a man of integrity. I was true, always, to what I believed.

Did I deserve to be the greatest? Did I deserve to use all my powers? Why not me? I found the answer to all those questions was *yes*.

A few weeks after my loss in Vegas, I went looking for entitlement, and I found it. Never again would I hesitate when it came time to do great things!

HONOR YOUR CODE, AND CREATE A HEALTHIER SENSE OF ENTITLEMENT

Each of us has a unique code. I cannot preach my code to the world, because it doesn't work for everyone. We all come from different religions, different backgrounds, different countries. We've been raised very differently, and the rules for how to live our lives are different, too. What our codes share in common is that each of us can move toward creating a better sense of entitlement simply by living up to them.

I suspect that you know what your code is, as does everyone. You may not have considered it or articulated it, but deep inside, you know it. Here is your call to action, and it's easy: spend *one minute* reviewing your code. Why? First, so that you know it exists, and second, so that you know what it is. I know my code; I live my code. And while my code may change over time, I'll continue to honor it.

PERSONAL CODE VIOLATIONS HURT ENTITLEMENT

I believe that the longer you live by your code, the higher your sense of entitlement becomes. I'm not preaching morality or ethics, but simply that you should live by your code, *whatever it is*, and understand that violations of it can lead to a loss of entitlement. Without entitlement, your odds of reaching success shrink.

Live by your code and give yourself a chance to say, "I deserve success. I'll accept success. I won't sabotage myself." Live by your code, and when the opportunity for success arrives, be it great or small, ask yourself, "Why not me?"

You can find an insightful video about how to increase your sense of entitlement at:

www.PhilHellmuthsPOSITIVITY.com

CHAPTER SIX

OPEN A DOOR

When I first moved to Silicon Valley, I kept hearing the same thing from super successful people: "I was in the right place at the right time."

At first, it sounded like modesty to me. Having found some success myself, and struggled with its challenges, I assumed it was what people said when they were trying to control their egos and keep their heads down (our topic for Chapter 7) .

But the more I heard people say it, the more I began to wonder. Deep in my mind, I kept peeling back the layers of the onion. What, exactly, did they mean?

Over time, I began to develop a theory: we are *all* in the right place at the right time, but most of us don't realize it.

MARTHA PLEASE PASS THE PEAS

Carl Westcott, a good friend and recipient of the Horatio Alger Award, hits the nail on the head with the following story. A man—I'll call him Jack—is at the dinner table with his family when he has a doozy of a business idea. Jack proceeds to lay his idea out for his wife, Martha, and his kids, who all listen closely.

He finishes explaining his vision, and a brief silence follows.

And then Jack says, "Martha, please pass the peas."

The point of Carl's story is that opportunity knocks all the time, but often we let it slip by while we focus on the triviality of life.

Now, imagine instead another man, Bill. Like Jack, Bill also has an idea. Both men, in fact, have the *same* idea: the dream of opening a sports bar.

Bill lays out his idea that night at dinner, just like Jack did. But unlike Jack, who goes to work the next day and forgets all about his dream ("Martha, please pass the peas."), Bill decides that tomorrow he's going to walk into his favorite sports bar and ask the owner a few questions.

When Bill meets said owner the next day, all it has cost him is a few minutes of conversation. But he's done something far more important: he has taken the first step toward his dream. He has, as I call it, *walked through a door*.

DOORS, DOORS, AND MORE DOORS

On the other side of that figurative door, there exist more doors for Bill—more forks in the path of life. More choices, more opportunities, and more possible steps. For example:

- Door one might be that the owner is sick of his bar and wants to sell it, and eventually helps Bill buy him out.

- Door two could be that the owner loves his bar—he's making money hand over fist—and he wants to start a second one, but he needs a partner to help him open it. Hello, Bill!

- Door three could be that the bar owner gives Bill good advice on financing, and that sends Bill through another door to bankers, which leads to more doors. Or perhaps door three sends Bill through a series of doors, and he hits a dead end, because he can't raise the funds to start a bar. But he moved forward, and when an opportunity comes up later, Bill's saved some cash, found a partner, or landed financing (more doors!) and he's ready to seize the chance.

- Door number four could be that the
owner tells Bill how much work it is
to own your own bar, and Bill decides
he doesn't want to work sixty hours
a week. In this case, Bill pivots to a
different dream.

There's an infinite number of doors in
this story, but it's easy to see the point: those
other doors are only available to Bill *after*
he steps through the first one. If he sticks
with "pass the peas" like Jack, he misses the
opportunity that's right in front of him; he
fails to realize that *he was in the right place at
the right time all along.*

Someone once said, "Take the first step,
and all manner of great things will fall into
your path to speed you on your way." It's
advice worth taking to heart; move forward
and open a door in your life. No matter how
small the door, open it, and ones to follow,
but always move forward!

BE READY TO OPEN YOUR DOOR!

It's my hope that the first five chapters of this book have been a call to action, and that you now have a good idea of what you want to achieve in life. More specifically, I hope that you now have a clear vision of your own dream, and are actively moving towards achieving it.

It's time to open a door. If there is no obvious door, give it a few days, always asking yourself:

- *What is the next logical step toward achieving my dream?*

- *What door can I open to move toward it?*

Remember: *you are always in the right place at the right time.*

CHAPTER SEVEN

HATE HURTS YOU

I n 2003, I was staking a professional player at an online poker site called Ultimate Bet. In poker, staking means that one person, the *staker*, puts up money on behalf of a player in exchange for a cut of the profits at the table.

In November, the administrators of the Ultimate Bet site called me to ask about unusual activity in the account of the player that I had staked. It seemed that the account in question had been drained when the player had lost $28,000 to someone else in four hands. In the "limit game" they were playing—where bets are capped—that was nearly impossible. It was clear there was a scam going on, and the player himself was involved.

I was shocked. So far, things had been going great with this player. He had been winning cash for both of us to split, and I was happy with the arrangement. Then, for reasons I couldn't understand, this "friend" had stolen from me by intentionally losing to another person who was in on the scam.

The whole incident was surreal. Had he spread the loss over 200 hands, he would have gotten away with it. But rather than pay three dollars per hand in rake, he took a shortcut and lost the money in four hands! Worse, and even more bizarre, he had indeed stolen $28,000, but *$14,000 of it was his money*. He could have just asked me if we could both withdraw cash, or just split the balance in the account. Not only was he a thief, but it seemed he was a terrible one, too.

Regardless, I was furious. And now I had to decide what to do. It was a situation that would put my #POSITIVITY mindset to the test.

HATE HURTS YOU

In 1999, my wife Kathy and I had studied Buddhism for a week with Lama Surya Das. I love the idea of forgiveness , and how powerful it can be. One concept in particular had really hit home for me: *hate hurts you*.

I'd had my own struggles with hate. Like everyone, I'd been wronged over the years—hurt by people I knew and trusted. My knee-jerk response in the past had been a deep resentment and anger toward them for having done me wrong.

Through my Buddhist studies, however, I'd learned to ask myself a simple question in these situations: *Who is being hurt?* When you answer that question honestly, you realize that it's you, as the *hater*, who feels the negativity and stress of the emotion. You're the one seeing red and feeling negativity every time you see or think of the hated ones. The hated people aren't the ones in pain, you are!

For the first hour or so after the phone call from Ultimate Bet, however, I was feeling anything but Buddhist. I was stunned, upset, and I was plenty mad. Not only had I staked this man, I had wired *more* cash to him the previous week so that he could put food on his family's table. I had done nothing but try to help him, and he had *stolen* from me.

I wallowed and stewed for a while, but eventually, I was sick of the negativity. I made a conscious choice. I thought, *I have a great life, and I choose to celebrate it. I'll take my wife out and go a little crazy. We'll spend a lot of money on a great meal and a nice bottle of Château d'Yquem.*

For the next few hours, that's exactly what we did. We had a wonderful evening, and I focused on all that we had, rather than stewing over what had been taken from us. While polishing off the wine, I decided that rather than take this public and have it get messy, I was going to bury it.

Later that night, I ordered all the people at Ultimate Bet that knew about it to keep it to themselves. Outside of Ultimate Bet, I only told two other people about it and swore them to secrecy. What good, I wondered, could possibly come from throwing mud around and destroying someone's reputation?

A THREE-STEP PROCESS FOR DEALING WITH HATE

It took more than a nice bottle of wine to reach a place of forgiveness, however. As I had developed my #POSITIVITY philosophy, I had come up with a three-step process for shedding my hate, and it has worked beautifully for me, and for my friends. Those few hours after the theft revelation from Ultimate Bet put that philosophy to the test, and it worked to help me find inner peace at a time when hate could have eaten away at me.

What follows are the three exact steps I use when I feel hate entering my life. You can use them yourself, even, and especially, for hate that you've been carrying for years.

STEP 1: PUT YOURSELF IN THE HATED ONE'S SHOES

Start by imagining the person that you hate the most in your life. Picture this person right now. Ready? The first step is to have a long, honest contemplation about *why* this person wronged you. Put yourself in their shoes. Try to understand why they did what they did. Let go, for a moment, and try to go through the same scenario as them. (In extreme cases, you may want to talk to a therapist to get help shifting your perspective.)

By putting yourself firmly in their shoes, you can begin to clearly see why they wronged you. In some cases, this step alone can reduce much of the hatred you feel.

STEP 2: FIND SOME GOOD IN THE ONES YOU HATE

Next, it's time to go a step further and strive to see the *good* in this person. Take a few minutes right now and ask yourself what positive qualities they might have. Are they charitable? Are they a good father, or a good spouse? Are they a good friend to others? Are they loyal? Can you find some goodness somewhere in them?

This isn't always easy to do, but with effort, you can always find *something* about the person that's positive. In one mean poker player's case, I focused on the fact that he was funny. That was all the good I could find in him, and it was weak, but at least it was something on the positive side of the ledger.

STEP 3: SEND THE HATED ONE LOVE

Choose a time when no one is around to disturb you. Turn your phone off. If someone else is at home with you, tell them that you need 15 minutes to meditate, and that they should not disturb you. Lie down, get comfortable, close your eyes and think of the person that you've held hatred for. With your eyes closed, see them clearly in your mind.

Now start sending love to them.

If you've never meditated, or "sent love," no problem, it's easy to do. However, sending love to someone you hate will feel counterintuitive and strange. But you'll be amazed to find your hate begin to melt away. It's difficult to send someone love and hate them at the same time.

A couple of months after I sent love to the gruff poker player I mentioned above, I ran into the gentleman and his attitude toward me seemed completely different. It was weird! I think he saw that my reaction to him had changed to become more accepting, and he reacted in kind. I played poker with him that night, and I found myself laughing harder than ever at his jokes. When he reverted back to form and turned his sharp wit on me to try to put me on tilt so that he could win my money at the table, I realized he had lost the power to negatively influence me. This was very the first time that I used the technique, and, just like that, a potential enemy no longer existed.

(Bonus: When I do this exercise at home in my bed, I can't help but send love to others in my life. After all, if I'm sending love to the ones that I hate, it seems to me that that I should send love to the people I love, too! I imagine my wife and my sons, my mother and my father, my sisters and my brother, and my best friends, and I send them love as well.)

FORGIVENESS PAYS?

After the theft at Ultimate Bet, I used those same three steps. I tried hard to see the good in the man who'd stolen from me, and I tried to understand where he was coming from—to walk in his shoes. Then—and I confess that this wasn't easy for me to do—I took an hour to meditate, and I sent him love. The effect was profound. I was amazed as a large portion of my hatred simply fell away.

One of the great side effects of having hatred vanish was the fact that I then had a sort of *void* where the negative feelings had been. In this newfound space, I found more room for entitlement, positivity, and love.

A few days later, I repeated the process. E ven more hatred fell away, and it ratcheted up my positivity even further. I found I was now more focused on the good things in my life—the blessings. They say that what you think about expands, and in my case, my blessings certainly expanded as my hatred dissipated.

Meanwhile, over the next few days, the two guys that I had sworn to secrecy were screaming bloody murder and telling me, "You should take this public! You should destroy this rat."

I kept telling them, "Forgiveness leads to good things."

How true that turned out to be.

10X RESULTS

A few days later, I found myself across the coast from my California home, in Foxwoods Resort Casino in Connecticut, to play in the $10,000 buy-in WPT (World Poker Tour) event.

If I had still been in the middle of a war over the theft, both in the Internet chat rooms and the poker world, or had I still been feeling strong hatred, I knew it would have affected my game, and there would have been no way that I could have lasted beyond the first day. I felt good about the progress I'd made.

Of course, walking down the hallway to the tournament room, I ran into the guilty fellow almost immediately. It was as if I were being tested. He was in tears, tripping over himself to apologize, and I knew that he was truly regretful. I shook his hand and accepted his apology.

I'm not going to say that it felt good to shake his hand. I still felt some betrayal and anger. But I wasn't feeling nearly the level of negativity that I would have had I not forgiven him, sent him love, and given up my anger by degrees.

I also would have struggled to play well. Had I gone public, like my friends wanted, then I would have crushed the guilty party on the Internet and spent untold hours answering questions from other players in the poker tournament room about how it all went down. I would have relived the incident over and over throughout the day and night. Instead, I kept my head down and focused on playing great poker.

I feel like I was rewarded for the way I handled myself. I went on to reach the final six and make the televised version of the WPT show. Eventually, I finished in third place for $280,000.

I couldn't believe it. It was *exactly* ten times what had been stolen from the Ultimate Bet account. With the $280,000 and the $28,000 numbers staring me in the face, I took it as a sign that forgiveness was the way to go, and perhaps far more powerful than I had previously understood. Forgiveness pays, or least it certainly did in this case! I knew that whenever possible, I would forgive people.

And why not? None of us have been perfect in this lifetime. We all make mistakes. I feel great about my life, but there are certainly one or two things I would take back, given the opportunity. Clearly this person made a mistake, and clearly, he regretted it. Still, I knew that the main reason to forgive him was that *I didn't want to suffer*. I forgave him for *my* sake. I didn't want to be flooded with negative emotions every time I bumped into him. I didn't want to see him walking towards me and feel compelled to turn the other way.

It was the right choice. And eventually, he paid me back in full. To this day, he protects me and defends me at any opportunity.

FORGIVENESS LEADS TO ... A FORTUNE?

The Ultimate Bet theft wasn't the only time that I felt that forgiveness paid dividends. Another gentleman consistently slighted me over an eight-year period. There was a budding rivalry between us, and he kept me out of the biggest and best poker game in Madison, Wisconsin. I'm sure he had plenty of good reasons to dislike me, including my "poker brat" behavior at the tables, but after leaving Madison permanently in 1994, I had no good reason to reach out to him and mend the fences.

Still, I called him personally to invite him out for an entire day in Santa Monica with a few others from the old Wisconsin poker gang. After that, things were good between us.

Things were so good, in fact, that he invited me to invest in the software company that built UltimateBet.com, which was interested in having me represent them. It turned out to be the most lucrative investment of the first 50 years of my life, by far. Ultimate Bet went public for $365 million in London, and when the smoke cleared I had made more than $10 million in cash.

The irony was not lost on me: one of my oldest "enemies" had invited me into the best investment of my life! Had I not mended fences with him, this opportunity would never have come my way . It was yet another reminder that I need to clear the air with, or completely forgive, anyone who slights or crosses me.

FORGIVENESS OF EXTREME ACTS

I have never faced extreme violence or the terrible acts of betrayal that many have. My perspective in this regard is limited. But one of my wisest friends, who has experienced more than a few horrors, has found great solace in forgiveness.

It's hard to see much good in a person who has committed a violent or heinous act. What helped my friend was to know that the perpetrator had been a victim himself when he was young. He now knows that there was something seriously wrong with the perpetrator.

It helped him to talk about with someone he had complete trust in (me; in fact, he hadn't spoken of it to anyone in ten years). My wise friend told me, "I benefitted by simply talking about it with you, Phil." It also helped him to talk about it with his partner. It helped him to know that he had broken the cycle, and that he had treated his own children well.

Can you forgive a monster like that, even if hatred feels like it is a form of protection and in your own best interest? It's challenging, but so are many of the most valuable things in life. I suspect that it can, at minimum, lessen the burden that you carry.

So, I say to you: forgive others, forgive their actions, and forgive their slights *for your own sake.* Someone may deserve to be hated, but you don't have to fall into the trap of actually hating them. Shed your hate. Like a snake with a crusty old skin, shed it! Leave the hatred behind, and move forward with more love in your life.

CHAPTER EIGHT

DEAL WITH NEW SUCCESS

A t the beginning of my poker career, I lost money on my first *ten* trips to Las Vegas. Each one was a blow to me, emotionally and financially, but I stayed focused and positive. Each time, I would rebuild my confidence, improve my game, and head back again.

During those tough times, I would often imagine the day when I finally won—I pictured how great I'd feel, how much easier it would be when I was a poker star.

I was in for a surprise.

When I finally won, I didn't feel very well at all. I felt almost physically ill.

At first, I didn't understand why. After all, this is what I'd wanted! Upon reflection, and the wise counsel of my mother, I realized that I was having trouble dealing with my newfound success. It simply felt unnatural.

Over time, as I started climbing the poker ranks, I grew more accustomed to winning—it began to feel far more natural to me. But there were still challenges to be faced as I accomplished more.

Hopefully, you'll have many new successes after reading *#POSITIVITY*. But be wary: a lot of sudden success can be more difficult than you might imagine.

If you're tempted to laugh at that, keep an open mind. Success, surprisingly, can sometimes be harder to deal with than failure—if you want proof, look no farther than the antics of the crazy celebrities! Just because you choose success, and set your sights on it, doesn't mean you're ready for it. Gay Hendricks covers how hard it is to deal with new successes in his book *The Big Leap*. Essentially, our nervous systems are hard wired to keep us in a narrow band of what we consider to be uncomfortable; new successes are just as uncomfortable to the nervous system as hunger, poverty, and the like.

LOTS OF PRAISE, LOTS TO DEAL WITH

As a celebrity, I'm regularly approached in public. Often, people come to me with praise. It's kind, and it's flattering, but in the past I struggled to deal with it. When someone offered praise, I would respond by trying to find a way to say something *not* great about myself—in effect, to deflect their praise.

I did understand at that point that too much praise could be a bad thing. But deflecting every comment with a self-deprecating one was like turning down a gift, and made everyone feel awkward. Imagine an excited fan coming up to me, and saying, "Phil, I love the way you play poker. In my opinion, you are the greatest poker player in the world." And I answer, "Not the way I've been playing the last two months, I'm not." It's disrespectful to *them*.

These days I simply say, "Thank you, I appreciate it." However, I try hard to not let the compliment all the way in; I try to not let my head swell. I want to acknowledge the person that gave me the compliment, but ignore it on the inside. I recognize that the person giving me the compliment is trying to give me a gift—I always shake their hand and accept their praise.

If you suddenly start to achieve success, you'll receive compliments and praise from family and friends, and perhaps the world in general. This can be very off-putting and feel quite unnatural. My suggestion is that you graciously accept the compliment, maybe even say, "Thank you, I appreciate it, I was in the right place at the right time."

I believe that many celebrities live their life based on external praise. If the world is praising their latest album, movie, sports success, or business success, then they feel too good about themselves. If the world is panning their latest efforts, then they feel too *poorly* about themselves. It's a trap I was caught in for decades.

THE COST OF MY MASSIVE EGO TRIP

In *Poker Brat*, I tell the story of how I left my room at the ARIA Hotel in Las Vegas to grab a take-out order at Javier's Restaurant. On the way out, I told my wife, "I think I'm going to run into Michael Jordan."

I knew MJ was in the ARIA Hotel as I had seen him two days earlier, and I just had a feeling I'd run into him. Sure enough, walking back to the elevators with my food, I spotted his huge form.

In Vegas, I walk *quickly*. MJ, however, was walking super slowly ahead of me. As I came flying up on him, I decided not to bother him. I'm a huge fan, and we had enjoyed a couple of meals together, but I knew he was probably stopped a hundred times a day. Instead, I slammed my sunglasses on, looked to my right as I flew by MJ, and nodded a quick, "Hi." Twenty fast steps later, I took a left-hand turn toward the VIP elevators, and 20 steps after that I took another left and pulled out my key to open the door to the VIP elevators. I glanced back in case I needed to open the door for someone else.

At his pace, there was no way MJ should have reached the corner yet, never mind the VIP elevator door, but there he was. Surprisingly, he had jogged to catch up to me. I held the door open and said, "Congrats on your wedding."

He said, "Phil, how are you?" And we had a few minutes together, which was nice.

The next day, I woke up to an email from a friend who said, "President Obama was in Palo Alto last night and was wondering how you're doing in the World Series of Poker."

That was enough to blow my head up completely.

Obama knows *me*? MJ jogged to catch up to say hi to *me*? I'm a bad ass! I'm so cool! All I wanted to do was tell everyone about MJ and Obama ... for *weeks*.

I was insufferable, on a full-blown ego trip, and it cost me. I had reached a record 99 World Series of Poker cashes, and was trying my hardest to get the historic 100th cash, but I had zero focus. For the next *sixteen days,* I missed that 100th cash--something which should have otherwise been easy to do if my head was right.

My 100th cash would have to wait until the World Series of Poker in Paris later that year, when my ego had deflated.

Don't be fooled. Managing praise, success, and heady stuff like hanging out with your heroes, is not easy to deal with.

IGNORING PRAISE

For many years, I had a bad habit. I would win a tournament and then get way too cocky. I would think I was great at poker and stop paying attention to the things that got me there, and then I'd proceed to lose a lot of money. Back in the '90s I wouldn't notice the mistakes I was making because "I was the greatest and I didn't make mistakes." Yeah … right!

It's no secret that I've struggled with my ego, and I've taken to looking to others for help. One person who seems to handle himself incredibly well is THE Elon Musk. He stays immersed in a one-on-one conversation, never looking behind you to see if someone else more important has walked into the room. Elon's ego is *not* out of control, not even remotely. I've have asked him on multiple occasions how he deals with praise, and his answer is always the same, "I ignore praise."

Elon keeps his head down and keeps moving forward. It's a great strategy, and it's one I wished I'd learned earlier, before my ego cost me millions of dollars!

TURN TO YOUR BLESSINGS

External praise is no shortcut to validation. When you need a boost, look to your Blessings list. Don't let the world and outside forces determine whether you're happy or sad.

If you're feeling a little too good about yourself thanks to outside compliments or praise, take a long look at your Blessings list. The very thing that you're receiving praise for probably isn't in the top three blessings on your list! I'm betting you have good health or good family above whatever it is that you are receiving praise for (probably business success). Keep things in perspective; if you want to feel good about something, feel grateful for your good fortune.

If I want to feel good about myself, my Blessings list cheers me up every time. And if I'm feeling too cocky I can take a long look at the list and feel good for the right reasons—ones that aren't about material success or adulation.

KEEP YOUR HEAD DOWN

Whenever I begin to feel too cocky, in addition to looking at my blessings for validation (and a smile), I try my hardest to simply keep my head down, figuratively speaking.

I take a long look at my yearly goals, and what I need to do to achieve them. *Keep your head down*, I remind myself.

If I'm thinking about achieving more, and what I need to do to get there, then at least I know I'm focused on the future and not focused on past successes or praise. *Keep your head down.*

I look at my Winning Pyramid and ask, "How am I doing? What do I need to do to get better?" *Keep your head down*, I remind myself.

MAKING IT AND THEN, WHOOPS, LOSING IT

They say that the average multi-millionaire has severe swings in net worth seven to ten times before they learn how to hold on to their cash. It's one skill set to make a lot of money, but another skill set altogether to hold on to it. The world of poker serves as an extreme lesson in this.

However you find your success, understand that these swings are natural and normal. If the money you make from your successes starts to dwindle, don't beat yourself up too much. Instead, understand that you have to search for new doors to open (like looking for better money management solutions!).

THE END ... AND THE BEGINNING

In 2018 I added a new entry to my Blessings List: I've raised $50 million for charity through tournaments that I (Linked Comment) emcee or host! There is a list of these in my autobiography *Poker Brat* and at PhilHellmuth.com.

Imagine how much entitlement this adds to my life (why not me?)! It's one of the great gifts of success: your success is a way to leave a legacy and help others.

In this book I've detailed eight of the strategies (tips and techniques) that have put me on my own personal path to success. I hope that the stories I've shared have helped you see that I've had my own challenges to face and overcome. My path is my own, but the strategies are something that anyone, anywhere, can implement to find their own way to a more fulfilling life.

Now, it's time for you to find your path—a clear path that you design for yourself. May the lessons of #POSITIVITY guide you on the way.

#POSITIVITY

- Write down your life goals
- Bathroom mirror your yearly goals
- Bathroom mirror your blessings
- Create your winning pyramid
- Honor your code
- Open a door
- Shed your hate
- Deal with new success

HOW TO GET MORE
#POSITIVITY

'm very much looking forward to the release of the sequel to this book: *#POSITIVITY 2: The Habits of 8 of the Most Successful People in the World.* In it, I'll show you how to move closer to your dreams by looking at the habits of high performers like Elon Musk, Jack Dorsey, Sheryl Sandberg, Chamath Palihapitya, Bill Gurley, Tiger Woods, Bill Lee, President Barack Obama, Jim Harbaugh, Tony Robbins, and President George Bush Jr.

In the meantime, here are several ways you can get more #POSITIVITY in your life!

Phil LIVE on ESPN
2017 World Series of Poker

#POSITIVITY KEYNOTE SPEECHES

In my #POSITIVITY keynote speeches, I show audience members how to open doors and think bigger. Speeches can be tailor-made to suit any audience, at any length, for any industry. For keynote and private consultation bookings, please contact my agent Brian Balsbaugh at Poker Royalty: (702) 868 9003.

PHILHELLMUTHSPOSITIVITY.COM

Visit www.PhilHellmuthsPOSITIVITY. com for a series of short videos designed to help you, the reader, do more! Each video delves deeper into the concepts in **#POSITIVITY**, and introduces new ideas that I believe will help you do more with your life.

I encourage you to visit PhilHellmuthsPOSITIVITY.com and upload your own positivity stories! You can help build a collection of thousands of inspirational stories from readers by sharing how you overcame obstacles to create new successes in your life.

On the site, you can also subscribe to receive monthly emails with my favorite inspirational quote. From Churchill to Gandhi, the Buddha to President John Adams, each email offers just one or two lines that will add a little more #POSITIVITY to your life.

#POSITIVITY COACHING

One of the challenges of super-success is how to deal with it! I look forward to helping super-successful people deal with their achievements without blowing themselves up.

Learn from someone who's been there how to deal with massive successes, how to keep your head down, how to ignore praise … and of course, how to deal with ego issues. That one's a well-earned specialty of mine.

For booking, consultations, keynotes, and media requests, please contact my agent Brian Balsbaugh at Poker Royalty: (702)-868- 9003.

ABOUT THE AUTHOR

Photo courtesy of World Poker Tour

Phil Hellmuth is a family man first and foremost, and lives in Northern California with his wife of 28 years. Phil has the following life goal: Become the greatest poker player of all-time. After winning a record 14 World Championships (and counting) at the World Series of Poker, Phil has achieved that goal! Phil is a New York Times Best-Selling author, a television commentator, a businessman, an advisory board member to two companies, and a tech investor. Phil truly wishes to inspire a global audience to become better, to think bigger, to do more, and to ultimately achieve their dreams...